MERE BEING

MERE BEING

Barry D. Amis

atmosphere press

Table of Contents

In Memory Of
B.D. and Sophie S. Amis
and
Debbie Amis Bell

Unprayered

Lately I've been eating what remains of almost,
wondering at the piercing empty of frayed endeavors,
the blackened simulacra of uninhabited backbone.

I stumble, go on, petitioner of misplaced imagine
seeking segments of coming out, of unexpected.

Intensified too-familiar misjudges, can't explain
the peregrination of self-circled lapis lazuli.
Blues travel sharpened density of wry angles.

Mock invocation billows like thin bloom, loosely
resurgent but sucking air. Cynics cackle.

Translucent neighbors look at me.
Their volcanoes of megabitching peal,
the pitched register of camp alarm falls incoherently.

Unprayered, I re-assemble the wail of pure patch quiet.
No one hears.

Pensées

These are the hours
and we are the vessels.
Clothe me in the full
trappings of *Paradiso*
or comfort me in
measureless dark
places. Each day's
suffering craves a
Beatrice. Each night's
gathering offers milk
and pudding. Waiting
is irrational. Athens
and Jerusalem debate,
heaven and hell am I.
The last dwelling
place summons,
humility and love
are the threshold.
About us these bones
strip, innocence lost.
The *terra mater*
of canceled days
terrifies.

Mine Own House

Onyx and obsidian
black death and black nativity

night is the path of two ways
the shadowing seducer

a fantasia of wickedness
vast   perilous   unrelenting
in a wilderness of complicity

where ballots of bullets elect

and blood rolls over us
lovers and executioners entwined

we
the interdicted and the obliterated
are born d.o.a.

that which is above and that which is below
are one

listen to the presences

deadly certainties
press the finite dimensions of flesh

earth devours her children
morning becomes shroud
homilies and harangues are anticlimactic

the dust of all things staggers

El Camino de Santiago

Scalloped Galician light
llama como una niebla que trae
deepening anticipation along
el camino welling with pilgrims.

Love of God takes in pobreza y
dolor like the epiphany of a raindrop
that nourishes the sanctum sanctorum
of this always unfolding precinct.

Beatitude es difícil y desde
el principio fissured gloom stamps
burr-crested ridges as trekking racks
the impermanence of body wearied by

tenaz viento y lluvia. El camino
disdains the hills and tips against clouds
as unscripted articulations balance on
the fingertips of the unknowable.

Night drops down, holds, surrounds
shadow's folded spell como si pudiera
hold back pressing mortality but still
we walk the road hacia el consuelo.

The Falcon and the Falconer

Old paradigms and Machiavellian scenes
    heaving at the edge of madness

intrude like passages from the *Book of*
    the Dead into Afghan light that rises

like the stealth leap of a snow leopard.
    Vulgar gatekeepers misread

the scrolls, injuring a language threaded
    through a maze of indecipherable masks.

We are the sacrificial fodder and *prima materia*
    of prepaid body bags, the handiwork

of Washington's weather. Fool and fruit
    breaking bad. Emperor Qin's army marched

into the afterlife. I'm looking for my freaking
    legs. Keep on going, sulphur and French

fries. What rages here is a journey through
    the underworld. Each day is the day

of judgment, each place is Hell. When I
    burn there is no phoenix, coming home is

reduced to atmosphere. Belled and soured
    wherever I am my tongue tastes dust.

Dust Thou Art

Even as green earth
creates marvels
life cannot defend itself.

Days of thorns
confect bitterness.

Piranha flesh
replaces what was
a tell-tale masque

and tears of eventide
heartbreak living.

Starlings declare beauty
in a mean old world
blooded blackblood blue.

For the South Side Dead

that argue
the ruthless cancer of blackbraced violence
and gales of anger-rapacity in full-blown blood streets.
Gangsta deadwill pushers and guilt stripped gun libido
shadowplague asphalt gardens that bloom
madhatter killer cokeasetic.
Homies hope for crack endowed escape velocity
amidst an endless expanse of eyelitter and drugs.
Still, things that living things cherish fall from our lives,
dumbstunned by bump being and territorial prerogative
so twistedly reality challenged and conscience-free.

A pall hangs over deathweaver gang dens darkly ruinous
that scar unruly days in heart-bruised neighborhoods
outraged by uncontrolled primeval self-assertion.
Brick-blocked and hard times chosen
store front pastors and tambourine saints
pray *rock of ages let me hide myself in thee.*

Behind locked doors and boarded up hope
a cacophony of sirens engulfs night's edge
as EMTs scythe through wounded darkness
and riddled lives.
Sable matriarchs, shrouded in sorrow, weep drug
driven catharsis, a black belt around their throats.

Impossible bronze, impossible ville.
Vexed everywhere dances dust,
bony down chest bullets,
ferocious dunning of ghetto swag,
the middle finger of God.

Hellish sensations seek conciliatory light,
the weight of carrying away coffins
so run-of-the-hood, goddamnit, time retreats.
Breathing and believing an unknown frontier,
our once loved sparkling wiped out,
this frame so out of focus,
goodwill so implausible.

Petra

Chambered in Nabataean dusk
otherness comes to a cul-de-sac
lovely of impossible architecture
cut in cliffs staggered of aftermath's tacit
residuum. Rarely can perception undress
beauty freed of wordless singularity.

Captive of something indiscriminate
the eye's elevation outstrips gutted ruin.
Veneration grips elusive grace
confirmed of whispers weighed in
rose-red dust obstinately rippled.
Behold, darlings, everything longs.

A Canticle for Hiroshima

Fuji-san   this morning rising
          escapes my heart.

A world snatched
                    the gone-missing   yet again
          the breath-taking purchase
                              of good and evil.

          Dust   raw and shapeless.

                    Selah.

We sail on ships of broken days
                    mendicant rubes   calloused by
          phony rituals
                    and theatrical times.

Upturned expectations   scream *a cappella*

          screw you! and banzai!

          At the border of unknown country
we find ourselves   ever unpleasant & tendentious
                    turning voiceless childhood
into unanticipated   boisterous   red rover boys
                              playing Vlad the Impaler

          in fey Whitechapel.

Flavors of *pinturas negras*

indescribable as disillusionment
            in San Luis Rey   where we
drunken conquistadors   fell into the abyss
        unafraid   but looking for
            the healer   of Lambaréné.

Thelonious Monk   at La Grotte Chauvet-Pont-d'Arc
        inscape cleanses   his *missa solemnis*
                wowing fans and penitents
            in gray and sullen concentration camps
with bloody Queen Mary
                executing the counterpoint.

How grand it was   to be Torquemada
        but his burnt offerings   play like toccata
and fugue
                at Andersonville and Treblinka
the western front of wild bunches
                and *Götterdämmerung.*
        Une saison en enfer.

Pagoda phantoms stalk   our mourned
            feng shui pursuit
                        of dawn no longer ours.

The relentless wheel turns   shaken, not stirred
            drawn into the great waves
                        off Kanagawa.

        They fell.

Mushrooms served.   Terror sealed.
        Houses farms flowers birds

                  salt   wine   and   water.
Balance and harmony pass.

                  So it goes.

                  Earth sorrows,
         among men the unimaginable.

In the seven folds of time
         the great white pelican   cries to the sea

                  robes of wisteria wither

         my eyes absorb the lethal clouds.

The moon in her nightgown
                  the soul's plaintive voice.

Round Midnight

and that sound last seen cached
in the cloud of lost monks cowled
in the mystery before all morning

hands held tight against shape-
shifting night the foul weather
born of syllables leaded of loss

queering morning as I dreamed
crescendos and diminuendos
the crane flew over my coffin

because I have ridden iron maidens
I have tasted this strange fruit
offered of the keys surrounded by

cat calls and horse shit hurtling
through hurt deep into doubt's labyrinth
where I prefer straight, no chaser

The Universe as Transcendental Illusion

Listening to Miles' *Sketches of Spain*
and thinking does God feel Don Quijote
does She get down with *Concierto de
Aranjuez* and chill when another nova
explodes or a black hole sucks up light
in spacetime we can't see in spite of
stars that wobble still we set out hoping
windmills are earthlike planets and
galaxies harbor friendly Spielberg E.T.s
Sancho drags his ass around this puzzle
but volatile Aldonza wants nothing to do
with this bitches brew meanwhile in her
digs God riffs on *Waiting for Manet*
aware that this 33 ⅓ is spinning to an end.

The Chapel Perilous

Shadow edges from portent to
Precipice. Time contracts.
Grueling impasse reverberates
As last days unsettle field and
Footing. *Lacrimae rerum*: each
Fallen day a small death.

Imbalance fatigues and emptiness
Is limitless. Time's gambit resides
In life's crime and everywhere
The best are consumed by fire.
Purgatorio becomes valediction's
Bloodbone exegesis and dark stair.

Night's bugle summons sacrifice
Beyond each threatening moment's
Dead-end flourish. I do not forget.
I do not affirm. Time is a covenant
And a torment, an old man's sham
Garments thrown down. I turn

Mindful of shadow before
Lilacs and violets astonish.

Black Bone City

Noir and shadow
                    wear chillingly
          a weightless unwillingly
of tomorrow's curtailment

down dumpster alleys
          urine and feces rally
rats and roaches explore
          limits of being

The homeless
                    rummage in refuse
dead souls
caned and unable
          comforted in cardboard shoes
                    looking for God in a wine bottle.

          The hangover of faith?
                    Determinism
                                        or wraith?

Demons and nightmares
reaches of madness

a sorrow of church sirens
Saint Judas and sinners.

Everything intuitions insensibility
          cosmopolitan hostility
          soup kitchens and shelters

indifferent cruelty.

In our bleeding
a poisonous seeding
crashing fragments of I believe.

Still   arbitrary remains come knocking
shuddering our breath

deep-bowelled night
                exposes God's city
        overdosing on meth.

        Sinister gifts
hearts and thews
a burning ashcan

                shameful ignominy.

Blue and Black

In the aftermath of bloodtongue
blue and black cleave from chaos
the debris of generations. Seeded
heart roars to life tipping unyielding
calumnies and seizures of language.
Shadowed places called home,
boneraw and pressed; the penury
of every day life so atrocious,
the damned downtrodden erupt.
Black, you see, is not a property
of light.

Exhaustion hovers inside and around
as it tumbles through rhetoric
and lamentation. Fear dangles in each
coming day and the indigestion of
oppression is powerful; the fragile
dance of clichéd theater, land minds
glimpsed. Attendant of can't-explain,
time-packed graves and wounds
are lowering. So much joydream
is lost that shadows hunch in tactile
uneasiness and weary pine.

Neurotic do-gooders fall back
downcast as they scrabble and
twitch in their collective guilt.
Rising blood searches for new hope
while we, immaterial flesh, astonish
the small-minded and self-important.
In a world of clumsy eyes & vanished
flock a door slams on unexpected

vowels, metaphors of blue and black
render great falls, the deep Sabbath
of unforced morning, silent witness.

Canyonlands

Dust settles. These cathedrals of
the desert, russet-colored buttes and
gorges, stretch across sere wilderness

where the Dirty Devil River palavers
and the land exerts its flung ruggedness.
A long-horned frisson stirs my grizzled

spirit so I pack away my Old Testament
God and take in the clan of Kokopelli.
The shy San Rafael cactus spurs me

through arches of cancellation where
this terrible strangeness says *mi casa
es su casa* and desert lessons remind

of being so that on this day, in this
place, nothing more is needed. Mesas
and canyons awash with peyote

wisdom prompt muddled feelings.
As I push along the old Spanish trail
memory chances on fortuity because

in this grandeur even the ancients
trembled and nomadic dust devils
spiritdance. Absorbed into rigid night

the lateness of body is no small thing.
I open to lost lore, erase the outside
world. Pictographs gather all my deaths.

Jeanne d'Arc

So it comes to this:
a mere lass
and her strange voices

whose enigmatic
visions we did
not envision

and faith too true
that flows like water
over parched souls

so that the people
dip their hopes
in this frail vessel

as princes tremble and
dare not countenance
such burgeoning.

Jeanne, you look
so small as the flames
lick at your holiness.

Clocking Down

The lazy at the center of me
orange motions icicle words
utterly thrashing contradiction
neverwhere of expected.

Elsewhere sloughed off
nights punctuate illusion flux
and grave stillness; unction
releases obbligato.

Outsides meaning aparts,
as it were, a last healing
ministered of dust.

Soon solitary in-seeker
burrows out. The un-theology
feral of clocking down.

Knifing Existence

Waiting is always or it is damnable
But it is never gospel. Night rolls in
Fleshless, without guarantee,
Buffeting hope. The urgent, undone
Jawing of concentrated hunger
Changes nothing. The blathering
Of wished-for suppresses the knifing
Existence of could-be. Still, beneath
Our shells, ghastly desperation feeds
Undone evening. Our desires turn to
Defiant, gray-muddled here. A howl
Of words escapes damaged truth;
Irritation urgent and inexplicable
Picks up. After the empty there is
No imperative. Flowers strewn and
Bouquets taken away. Coaxing
Spirits huddle, mindlessly repeating
Themselves. Nothing to be done.

Lost Horizon

Sailing between poetry and despair
the convocation of hazard chastens.
Out of fold and foible the grip of amplitude
yields to the freshness of outward things,
the open sea deep in acrobatic paradoxes.

November's body is not an argument.
Flawed conception bedevils our troubled
mythology of abstraction pent in seasons
of infelicity where we, bier-borne mortals,
fall naked into fathomless waters.

I tend toward improbable in the absence
of divine. Others gaze upon God,
the syllabus of salvation hieroglyphic.

Drifting toward shadow I pursue
the bottom of tears and swim in
the dormant upward of dropped faith.

We won't be saved.

We

Who sin down ages
In discomposure that renders
Gone only find piety mocked,
A charade of innocence.
The letting go
Sulked by day's shadow.

Too tomorrow
That neither thought nor eye avail.
Truth become brittle,
Guilty innocence kicking.
Fake currency and dalliance hours
Another unthinkable.

Unseen soon-to-be tempers
Dumped sadness,
Heavenhell's grave cudgel-
scripted *mise en scène*.
God fatigue and pretense
Call *not so fast*!

Paths Unsettled

Unexpected matter-of-fact deaths
of invisible men
      if you dare *hold these truths*

flummox rudiments of hope.
Yet something blooded impels
a way that would forthcome
the fire next time

after which Uncle Tom's children
Nat Turner
      Harriet Tubman
            Rosa Parks

remember
centuries of ghosts
slave ships and plantations
hanging trees and Jim Crow
and fashion a station
of brothers and keepers
that frees paths unsettled.

The genius of belief cast
so that   even we
    in this place   can see

that matter
    those lives
      what black
is.

Céide Fields

Alone, where moon was meant
to touch day, the sound unfolds
from Lascaux to city lights
pasturing through words
of pentimento and moods of
chiaroscuro, a glorious song
of skylarks haunted by Neolithic
henges and dolmens.

Remembering of place and
pleasuring before language
apocalyptic fire snares the awful
white goddess, breaks the spirit
of Céide Fields. In exhaustion
and regret she flees the iron plains,
scarred by the blindness of stones
and bitterness of mouths.

Fugue in April

Alabaster worms & bird droppings scent edgy kabbalah
      Mary Jane and I cavort in the healing fields
littered with any number of equicollateral sarcophagi
      festooned of cancerous skincrow sweat-lusting.
Metaphorical fugues strange loop the grammar of DNA
      all conformations cuing a superconductive cycle.
Multiple recursive structures bebop arcing apotheosis
      as bum *homo habilis* patterns dusk-laden landfill.
Ironies of afraid drown murdered springbird laughter
      boom boom boom soon tra la la la la the hit man
In furious absence livid thereabouts gangbang truth
      ejaculating propriety tired of yesterday's whore.
I enter my PIN into her ATV, the harvest fertile
      and rhythmic. The dead sit up, glowing.
Spectered moon dogs break away. Unafraid at last.

This Place In

The rooms of life are much unlike the looms
of night, tight in their unspaciousness where
unwoven tapestries hang in dreams too big,
cloistered in days too brawny.

Unable we came from the grungy stable.
Come moon, come heartbeat. Cratered
images complicate this conceit complicit
of unrequited hopes dimmed in starry cast.

In grained parlors, cloaked as hours,
prayers cloud promised blessing. Deep we
fell becoming mere form dependent on

heart's pressing. Dazzle collapsed. There was
no end. We lugged faith without within,
lost or not this place this place this place in.

De Profundis

Sky falls into me
tendrils interwoven,
poised sinew
looking for bloom.

Earth is a hard journey
every detail leeches blood,
the Chronicles of Evil
hearken torment & tomb.

Morning slips by in ages,
the cost of grave fusion
whose destined ghosts
ferment fiber pain.

The heart found deep,
sextant and pole star
of vanishing life force,
too late to hold night's nerve.

Lording dwellers dumb of
pattern's breast brook
furtive dilemma that
keeps script and death.

Wayfarers

Hesitant communicants
trek the long road
scant of faith stations,
the waybill full of
mysterious geometries
and elusive harmonies.

Disoriented spirituality
& contrition grieved by
counterfeit script's
delicate moments
concede layers lost
& deceitful nuance.

The fragile edge
exposed.

Demon Air

Among the fierce griefs and insidious wounds
found in the usual dark places and nameless
neighborhoods, where days of strife kick ass
and fraternity loses its connotation,
throwaway society's dregs are fractaled
by pathology and demon air.

Disinherited ghetto inmates plunge into
depths of rottweiler anger. Rage provoked
by bitchblasted accusers and abusers
who manipulate this shadowspirit world
of resident hopelessness that is coded
in quenchless narcotic gloom.

Gloom that absorbs the blasphemy
of black and the stench of contempt
swollen by chronic bullshit. We are
forever newborn victims repeatedly
the other side of grace. Offspring of
sin sent normality cloaked in subterfuge.

Atonal

Trolley tracks straight to Hell
run deep into horror's grotesque   *Ni más ni menos.*

only which I ever expected
to genius   *Burn city boy!*

where bleeding you have sinned
you never whole again   *Where you gonna hole up?*

beyond surreal rites unfocused
psychedelic stupor   *Dusk of dust.*

whose scenes and ghosts
fears and graves   *Death-howling.*

blood-scarred my
slashed eyes   *There are no tears.*

insisted
in a thousand whys   *Soon banalities.*

watching back
living in spite
of   *Le temps perdu.*

Yardbird

songbirds full of yard confirm
bird watchers unjust friends
not heroes or heroines
blue notes birding

saxophoning gossamer riffs
where once insistent warning
warming goes else where
sins dare

fate
depths dimension
shatters images in its aches

birds away telling moody truth
unbelievable chords swoop
to flourish down

found time

Elegy

Age stumbles in sober imperium
Blistered and bandaged,
A conjuror of fantasyscapes whose
Scales of substance, sapped and
Out of kilter, are overtaken by
Marrowed incertitude.

Framed as unconsummated art
Life looks back and goodness is
A perilous path. The barren life
Discombobulates. Death is a holiness
We cannot love. Staying not a choice,
Paradox without remove.

A peculiarity of innocence animates
Romantics and martyrs who
Entertain choreographed angst
That panglosses remarkable All,
Not as figurative abstraction but
As vestige of something forfeit.

Temples, Tabernacles, and Tablets

In temples of the but-for
dark is a mood
      that collects itself

The wolf carries me
      to after-hours of estrangement

an upward struggle
      tearing abeyance apart

This way and that way are gone

Whatever fell from the sky
I fell from healing
      the shape of fluent grief

Shadow climbs from my void
      fluster spreads

The conviction that I am otherwise
      irrational

Conjugations of sheep
      bear no by and by

Innuendo veins my disorientation.
      Bastions of caricatures undone
      jostled by the taste of hurried fruit

A splinter of hovering
        disquiets earth's rituals
the ineluctable vessel unleavened

        Say it,
stone is no substitute   for manna

Opioids

I
Cracked
The world is heavy
Breath a flutter.

II
Release
Toe'd up
The dead at rest.

III
Beware!
Lotus-eaters
The invited guest.

Las Alturas

High in the Altiplano,
tousled of wind and light,
swirls a song of fire and
ice whose complex rhythms
and rustic ambiance interplay
with troublesome ancestors.
Lacerated surroundings comb
the cordillera that messages loss.

Chattering cold and warp
dapple time-sheared expanse
with spellbound charge. A
crevasse gouges, stone trees
offer communion. Random
patterns hallow as restive
angst spills beyond the pale
smile of wrinkled clouds.

In this world beyond the world
solitude and shadow agitate.
Llamas and chinchillas, flamingos
and salt lakes decline to much
astonishment as inexplicable
presences grip plain and plateau.
Earth and hushed breath brace
for raw exploitation.

Guernica

death dowager
vein speared
horn of my wound
daggers my panic
all bulb-eyed and
horse terrified
white bull black
entr'acte
orchestrated pain of
chaos-cum-carnage

Heraclitus Visits the Wasteland

I went to where the path began
but where it was,
it was no longer.

No longer am I he who was but
a stranger in a world shut of eyes

filled with time-packaged
shadow where light obscures
and the clock turns slow.

Other times spilled to faithloss,
all forms forfeit. The attrition of
paradise and horizons sore,

the comfort of resurrection
problematic.

Innocence fled the pathless fields
where joydream withered
and ruin deepened.

Numbness grew in heart's center
and hues of hurt touched us,
our only days grown old.

Storms and fashion tumbled
through rhetoric and intercourse.

In time untamed,   unfathomable   fire.

Black Sun

There are many ways that it could end
but if it has to end perhaps not knowing
is not an insufficiency but intelligible
only when eager inquisitors apprehend
mere upset postured as mortal sin golden
moments whose reason impugns our
once and only wellwanting grief
thinned of possibility telling release
lost energy of the faceless gone duped
by fingerprint runes agile assumptions
succumb to long ago foreboding in
fields where birds did rise and hum.

Cursed Is the Ground

between cross and crescent
that harbors hardened disciples
couched in flesh, deep in blood
quite dispiritedly archetypal.

Woe Jerusalem! Dubious works
trough in shroud-shadow,
the scourging instrument
of this sepulchral cattle.

And there, gashed and
exhausted by immutable tissue,
prolonged obliquity accrues no
deft surcease, no hidden release.

Lacerated. There is nothing.
Vultures pleasure on carrion.
All this affronts Elohim,
lamps of this cursed land dim.

B L M

Tangled black fortitudes
staccato lacerated
broken windows and vacant hearts
perforce derelict of mercy.
In night brief presence
I dawn
outsized behavior
        aggrieved disrespect
a young man attired
        provisional
                articulate.
Black Sisyphus
susceptible to
zeitgeist
        demoralization
                destruction.
Even so
I do not
take refuge
        run away
                implode.

Freedom's Captain

Unconquerable purpose undone
Trap door sprung — in God's grace he hung.
"Oh Mary Don't You Weep"

Half slave, half free
Irrepressible conflict guaranteed.
We've "been buked and scorned" too long.

Wickedness roils cotton's domain
Dry bones cry out in anguished refrain.
Oh the souls gone home.

Golden Rule in demise
An angry God's sinners we chastise.
For suffering & humbled flesh trying qualm.

Union an ominous fate
Slavery, murder, terror, and lynch law
Are Babylon's tragic flaw.

Stymied by pacifism
And ruthless ruffians in their midst
Dark days and fury draw a determined Calvinist.

Pilloried and praised
Of another time he left friend and foe amazed.
Valor and act "Go Down Moses"

Into the maelstrom
Blood & bodies beyond sensibility
Excites the wrath of God at Pottawatomie.

Ethiop bears the weight
At the Hallelujah meeting before Heaven's gate
"In That Great Gettin' Up Mornin'"

A simple meal
With ghosts of Gethsemane.
Will the darker brother ever at the table be?

Grim-geared riders ponder
The drift of Shenandoah's unmourning waters
flowing past slave quarters.

The ferry fight futile & notorious,
Unjust actions "make the gallows glorious."
"Gone to be a soldier in the army of our Lord."

If Kingfishers Could

Only if kingfishers could
In their bright shyness
Quicken halcyon days
Reconciling the fall.

Then those days would light upon
Nameless streets & uncharted hearts
And among ashes and betrayals
Men would hear the baby's cry.

In our slow womb of stark lasting
Troubled of tongues that
Traffic between fire and water
A grace costly in flesh.

Look Away, Look Away

This is the was
of a world opaque,
uncomforted in gods
the core disintegrates.

Tall heavens taunt,
faith crumbles,
identity flees,
psyche & essence bleed.

Shapers of flame face
fierce voices and feelings,
surreal oddments
stripped of healing.

A ruthless finality apt,
fruit in the trees
blood on the roots,
absolution trapped.

Days of dismay
everything collapses.
Darkness that haunts
yields no perhapses.

At the end of amen
these bones adumbrate
caprices of flesh
in some elseplace.

Edge of the Mirror

We savor of waves too sorrow
the tenuous wake of
consequence and attitude,
the alchemy of self-frightened narcissistic conjunctions,
tambourines banging away.

Clichéd mint juleps and vacant conviction,
notorious conciliatory nonsense,
noise and negativity,
grief plagued addict-anchored opiate moon in water,
mime-suggesting portrait.

The slow dross of crooked crank,
shade at my feet,
unanswered and transitive.
Swift zeitgeist death-delighted puppet habitude,
this very jester jabberwacky.

Darkness Upon

Lost in my own life   grace unravels
          subtle folds of anxiety
        weave nightmares and *bêtes noires*
the never-never predicament odd and insidious.

Emotional vortices   thread dubious embrace
        unknown paths and deceitful passions
              dance in oddity
        every out of place.

Numbing depths of meaninglessness
        sincerity   so thin
        one could rightly inquire   what the hell?
              Day and night rain
        the thirst of waking self-evident.

        Solitude and sorrow
              flaunt unexpected strength.
  Understand my breath
              fire exuberant allows
                        death pulls.

We are hunger-gatherers   men and women of rage
              recompense sapped
                    a way of life jacked.
        Virgins and dreamers won't be awakened.

Of love and light
              is there such a kingdom?

Our Night, Our Noir

I heard the night
full of tears and tempest

Grieved by troubled measures
doomed transitory

grotesques and gall
fiendishly acerb

driving irony and temper
through breaking hours

a plenitude of put-downs
prodigal of light

drawn to
nettle or nothing

that informs our
chagrin-anchored hurt.

Shadowscent

In the day and night of the heart
auroras of magical turn toss
the salad of our supper with
croutons of myrrh and dashes
of sage. Living spices the entrée
of our intense repast that lasts too
briefly, faltering in petulant gloom.

In the summer of thyme we picked
the fruit of illusion and danced an
intoxicating antipasto of dreams
and protests where flowers were
children and love was free. In life's
frolic all we wanted, as Aretha
said, was some R.E.S.P.E.C.T.

From tenements of fleshlessness
we grew in storms of altered times.
We never expected *la vie en rose*
but the moon's hook draws days
to a close and leftovers salt doubt,
our summer days more arrested
development than *fait accompli*.

60th Reunion

A gaggle
of old men

remnants
of youths past

whose autumnal
demeanors

appreciative
yet gut punched

etched by ephemera
and humbling absences

embrace bonds of
fraternity and memory

life's audacious palette
still central.

Angst

I am so bent.

Tangential thoughts,
nonchalantly irrational,
escape these days.
Fractured variations of light
close in.

More ominously
blood and hours pour,
no purchase received.
Love and mythology drift,
the wild cudgel of survival
freaked with pale visions.

In the hollow,
decorated by oak leaves,
a faraway God shuns me.
My heart lets go,
stunningly whiplashed

and there is nothing.

Blackshadow

I

On a killing morn
   A loss, a sorrow
Dumb at dumbness
   Reason hollow.

II

Of the absurd
   Pitch broken
A blackshadow maze
   Where fallen is token.

III

Treacherous days,
   A fragile frame.
Medium or blood
   Thirst beyond change.

Suicide of the Soul

Eden's bewildering forfeit
was always too much.
Broken unlovely,
bruised and foisted,
witnesses how loss fell.
Misunderstood anima,
rendered scary,
weighs fatuous limits.

Surfeit shortcomings
fierce in images,
deep dark matter,
and ample grief
flail mulish flesh
whose frailty of faith
and startled piety
damn.

Grace founders
neither folly nor follower.

Freewheeling in the night
God sputters.

Surrealism in America

This tilted world pin balls. Ethical
brothels disconcert as cynicism and
fashionable shibboleths intercourse.

Strange-cast justice and Jim Crow's
long goodbye trouble. Day is decoyed,
many suns lost; long seasons that cost.

Uneasy acquaintance. Serpent progeny
shadowkeeps. Black sojourners and
awkward truths metaphor.

Blood marks and absurdities characterize
bad ideas' broad surround. Faux regret
and odd words pose as common ground.

Crimes of the heart tell everything: effigy-
clichéd reflections hang in museums
of the mind, myth agents of long libel.

Repair Me Now

        I walked in dark places,
from which I never expected
to return
        where once you have been
blood spills
        and spills again.
Death comes time-screaming
        in hopeless terrain
named and nameless
where absurd exorcisms appall.

        The century was reckless.
We spoke in tongues of our time
        gulag   mujahedeen   blitzkrieg
kamikaze   desaparecido   apartheid
                intifada

        T.S. said it was a waste land.
Somehow I avoided traumatization,
        crossed the Styx
hell-bent on the path that led to
        Robben Island and Montgomery.
I was messed up for a while
        but Rosa said sit down and
we stood up.

        All that exploded in dark ceremonies:
John, Martin, Malcolm, and Bobby
carried away in boxes.

        The headlines were
My Lai, Srebrenica, and Rwanda.

When the brothers came home
I was down there reading names on a wall,
remembering faraway places,

the relentless foe still inside me.

Lady Day

i.
This morning, this day of paradoxes
has an incandescence,
a holiness in each breath

that frames frailty and failure,
immense talent and darkness,
and things which are unsung but true.

The music understands that
it is possible that the compass of hurt
is leaning towards God and

conscience dwarfs the difference
between tragedy and failing,
but these images are a heaviness.

ii.
Wear me lightly, gentle humanity,
like a child that is desire,
a sorrow that is essence.

And be kind, indifferent days,
flesh is fragile and
nothingness will outlast the sacred

because night is a ripple,
the transcendent harbor we will know
when we know innocence.

Grace

Elliptical light divines
coincidences of lavender
in ritual imagined
remnant-running flesh.

Shadow falls away
in scent madness,
our path gossamer
lost among tombstones.

Mystical whence
folds in subtle camber;
skull or loins
sackcloth will more.

Time reaches in.
The world shorn of holy fire,
diaphanous and hollowed,
carries to no end.

Lost of direction
zenith contingent
groombride breath
kisses night.

The Gates of Hell

Walking around the 27th floor of a six story building
pain-splattered by cries of anguish
anarchic memories gather
memory now memory forward omnipresent draining
a drop by paradox mumbo jumbo slow motion emotion
thoughts past   images present   always
contrary free feeling hornet's nest haze-distortion
stars fall   night gasps   long past shadows reach
the cycle of ruin fully at hand

so the far end
a forfeit in our avenues byzantine
if this life
          unwise in plagues
                  has any meaning at all
crosstown riffs   burning guitar   flash back
brilliant flames in the jaws of demons
voodoo psychedelic
both sides of the sky not enough
what an experience   Jimi

time and time
beguiling registers of music mystery   misery
impenitent lonely heart   user shredding
ghost shadow buried in blues
the unimagined urgency of troubled times
wounds   pieces of life   big brother looking down
thinking about going home
it makes me cry baby   Janis

I, I, I am was will be echo thunder and question
trenchant turbulence overwhelming   undermining

where have yours   mine   ours
perception   heaven   hell
doors slammed   fires lit   some wild shit
people are strange
couldn't get much higher   Jim

never mind grungy   drugged   struggle   spleen
looking for love and nirvana things happen
argue   pretend   deprivation   turmoil
these are
            these are the
                    are the fog
                            are the feeling
                                    the unknown
feeling fueled   head full   unnerving maze
life walks away
no apologies   Kurt

enormous bee hive-assertive angst
palliative depression
see my stripped of   hold your one last time
trouble sailing endless downtrodden
self-willed collage calamity   main attraction
scratching   barfing   neon encore   fool's paradise
rehab ain't ecstasy
the newly dead ain't a game
the songs are done   Amy

unscene sense whispers not since presences
were-eyes ideas   susceptible   deep currents craving
jawed outcome   property building   graffiti
down street   same old bizarre
branded thinkthought   letting go   voice sorrow
oracle dichotomies crowned
devil at the door   Basquiat

culled nameless notes coagulate
symptomatic particulars expanding absence
griefs not alone
this world   this whirl
insecurities   resentments   flourishing evil
a lexicon of normalcy so foreign
collective rewards of virtue uproarious
enigmatic pretenses   indistinct dimensions
understanding not understood
privileged contradictions unburied
essential wonder refuged in darkly
dopes dupes victims
how   how   howl
souls empty

Moai

In the empty ocean cast far away
And alone Easter Island is a speck.
The ancient Moai turn their backs
On the sea, look inland, if not inward,
At the strange vicissitudes of taunting
Morning and boisterous ocean.
Homesick for vanished forests, palms,
Petrels, and cormorants, broken by
Dread centuries of rats, missionaries,
Slavers, and disease, they are inured
To caprices of unexpected convergence.
These silent sentinels like so much else
Have fallen, but on this island nothing is
Simple. Each noble figure is a construct
Of heartache. Lie down my guardians,
We go to meet miracles.

Over and Above

There were some things that only time could cure.
Arthur C. Clarke, *Childhood's End*

Carnaval in the sky, gateway of wonder,
a noggin-boggling pandemonium of azure,
magenta, opaline, & saffron will-o'-the-wisp
colors that drag our discovering upward
to gotta go spirit and provenance,
zenith and nadir, a cauldron of creation
where palette-scattered rosettes of pearls
samba across Corona Borealis sky, lamp
of our darkness, pantheon of deities
as black Orpheus sings "A Felicidade."
Our dislocation, our works and ages
thrown down, humbled, flung into fire.
Blue planet lost.

We enter young star clusters
calling the other within, causal paradigms
flaunted as galaxies and worlds, constellations,
comets, meteors, messengers, legends, utopias.
Gabriel and Ezekiel herald Earth's dawn,
a surreal kaleidoscope of cosmic calisthenics,
a daunting new alphabet.

Being and grace, the fruit of life assembles,
feast days and powerful images,
jumping the moon.
Lyrical heavens, impossible worlds,
inevitable yet enigmatic –
peculiar destiny, undiscovered possibility;
human fantasy
so simple and complex.

And then
loop quantum dreams that hoist and harbinger
mystery and mysticism, red giants and cat's eye,
dark energy, heavy elements, singularities;
the virility of martyr attributes setting free
hollow rituals of time in the transformative
womb of genesis and imagination.

Ark. Pegasus. Pole star. Time Lords.
Necromongers and the Underverse.
Deep-throated death-running outworld of
covens of black holes and fated apocalypse
washing over present flesh, flesh of memory
dumb in our verity, mourning our not.

Magnitude and incongruity push on,
fetish and phoenix pored over.
The cryptic out, out palpitating abyss
gathering deeper, wandering heaven,
beneficent elements of sacred force
strip away the inessential.
Andromeda clusters and nebulae
gardens an unrelenting what if.

In the grotto of universal yearning,
dream catchers and shivering angels ablaze,
in the throes of wonder-inspiring sacrament
these celestial landscapes launch
base matter's no win hope to escape.

Chariots and TARDIS. HAL 9000. Stargates.
Enormous time. Interstellar *pas de dieu.*
Supernovas, mandalas, and matrix labyrinths,
oracle & axis give expression to the insubstantial.
Yin and Yang matter-stunned,

Daedalus and Icarus, E.T. and Yoda,
heretic sky and coffin sea embraced,
sadness inverted, the gifts of gods untouched.
Cosmic runes, grail and spear of our selves,
so far out, so terribly endless.

There
        Then
                Ever
Every subtle thing cradled.

Note: Inspired by the Hubble Space Telescope images
of the Westerlund 2 star cluster in the Milky Way.

Our Times

In an age that barks
I know not about quietude and serenity,
a conciliatory frontier
footprinted in the outskirts of memory,
become in letters of time
a lexicon of existential calamity
whose translations of hate-holding
eclipse the heralded
in a befall of our finitude
that images presentpast conundrums
this dustshadow unlike ...

Perils time downfalls
deathdying hooded sky
reality unworthy
as seasons and congress, malice attired,
bruise here where God doesn't
and so the moment bristles,
tattered in brier Levis
whose jaws-locked young note miscreance
even as multiple currents
argue loaves and legends
churning proclivity ciphers, though lately ...

Each Day

each day is a calculus
        gather beautiful
                point to "like so"

explain fearcutting
        and try donor words
                a favorite is deliverance

weep forbidden and
        open obsessive curtains
                the surprise of only awaits

taste stillness
        and cradle illusion
                inexplicable will blossom

when outside mixes in
        water spaces in the heart
                the trick is Paris

then cactus and firefly
        unknown unknown
                articulation will be fine

wade into impossible
        expedite understanding
                speak music

About Atmosphere Press

Atmosphere Press is an independent, full-service publisher for books in genres ranging from nonfiction to fiction to poetry, with a special emphasis on being an author-friendly approach to the challenges of getting a book into the world. Learn more about what we do at atmospherepress.com.

We encourage you to check out some of Atmosphere's latest releases, which are available at Amazon.com and via order from your local bookstore:

Let the Little Birds Sing, a novel by Sandra Fox Murphy
They are Almost Invisible, poetry by Elizabeth Carmer
Spots Before Stripes, a novel by Jonathan Kumar
Transcendence, poetry and images by Vincent Bahar
  Towliat
Mandated Happiness, a novel by Clayton Tucker
Time Do Not Stop, poems by William Guest
Adrift, poems by Kristy Peloquin
Dear Old Dogs, a novella by Gwen Head
Bello the Cello, a picture book by Dennis Mathew
Auroras over Acadia, poems by Paul Liebow
Ghost Sentence, poems by Mary Flanagan
*Love Your Vibe: Using the Power of Sound to Take
  Command of Your Life*, nonfiction by Matt Omo
*Leaving the Ladder: An Ex-Corporate Girl's Guide from
  the Rat Race to Fulfilment*, nonfiction by Lynda Bayada
How Not to Sell: A Sales Survival Guide, nonfiction by
  Rashad Daoudi
*Letting Nicki Go: A Mother's Journey through Her
  Daughter's Cancer*, nonfiction by Bunny Leach
That Scarlett Bacon, a picture book by Mark Johnson
Such a Nice Girl, a novel by Carol St. John

About Barry D. Amis

Barry D. Amis lives in Alexandria, VA and has degrees from Penn State, the University of Pennsylvania, Middlebury College, and Michigan State. He was professor of American and African American literature at Michigan State and Purdue University. He was also Fulbright professor of American Studies in France, Madagascar, Cameroon, and Niger. He lectured and conducted workshops for the United States Information Agency in more than two dozen countries in Europe, Africa and the Middle East. He was a Regional Director for the Association for Supervision and Curriculum Development (ASCD) in Virginia. His poetry and articles have appeared in a variety of journals.